Software Testing – A Complete Handbook

Lakshmi Narayani

© 2012 Lakshmi Narayani

All rights reserved. Except as may be permitted by the Copyright Act, no part of this publication may be reproduced in any form or by any means without prior permission from the publisher.

Limit of Liability / Disclaimer of Warranty: While the publisher and the author have used their best efforts in preparing this book, they make no representations or warranties with respect to the accuracy or completeness of the contents of this book and specifically disclaim any implied warranties of merchantability or fitness for a particular purpose. The advice and strategies contained herein may not be suitable for your situation. Neither the publisher nor the author shall be liable for any loss of profit or any other commercial damages, including but not limited to special, incidental, consequential, or other damages.

Acknowledgements

Thanks to everyone that encouraged me to write and publish: R.L. Narasimhan, Meenakshi Narasimhan, Sujatha Srinivasan, Srikanth Ranganathan, L. Sundararaman, C.M. Krishnaswamy.

Thanks to o Shantha Ranganathan and Ramanan Gopalan for their support when it was most needed.

Special thanks to Pushpaben Patel for taking care of my daughter while I wrote the book and to Mahima Srikanth for being my greatest inspiration.

About the Author

Lakshmi Narayani is an IT Professional working for a multi-national IT company. She holds a Master's degree in commerce and has worked in the IT industry for 14 years. She has donned many testing roles from being a Tester to Test Delivery Lead over these years.

She has also been the instructor for various training courses on Software testing when she worked for EFunds International. Her paper on Test Script reviews was published in the 5th Annual QAI Conference. One of her articles was published in Better Software magazine.

She has also published many e-books on various software testing related topics and also rhymes and educational books for children.

About the Book

This book is intended to be a good foundation on Software Testing concepts and processes for an aspiring or a novice tester, or anyone that wants to venture into the very interesting field of Software Testing to learn the basic tricks of the trade. Usage of jargon or complex principles and techniques has been intentionally avoided to make it easy to read and easy to comprehend. The author has been a Software Testing practitioner for many years and everything that is included in this book is directly coming out of the practical experience gained over the span those years.

Chapters 1 through 4 explain the very basic concepts and definitions of Software Testing, the systems, the key players and the Software Testing Life Cycle phases.

Chapters 5 through 12 elaborate on the test phases and the processes and tools every tester should know about along with some examples and process flow diagrams.

Chapters 13 through 15 contain some practical wisdom on topics like defect detection techniques, how to write effective tests for GUI objects and how to become a successful Tester.

Chapter 16 has useful exercises on the topics covered in the book to confirm and reinforce the concepts covered in this book. Solutions or answers have not been provided intentionally – that would make it way too easy to skim through and forget. To verify whether the answers are correct, it is recommended to go back and re-read the relevant chapters.

Contents

Chapter 1:   Introduction 1
    1.1   Who can become a Software Tester? 2
    1.2   What is Software Testing? 2
        1.2.1   Quality of Software 2
        1.2.3   Requirements 3
        1.2.4   System/Application 3
        1.2.5   Errors 3
    1.3   Recap 4

Chapter 2:   All about Systems 5
    2.1   Front End 5
    2.2   Mid – Tier 5
    2.3   Back End 5
    2.4   What is a database? 6
        2.4.1 Relational Database Management System 6
        2.4.1.1   Tables 6
        2.4.1.2   Fields 7
        2.4.1.3   Records 7
        2.4.1.4   Database Query 7
    2.5   Recap 7

Chapter 3:   Know the Players - SDLC Stakeholders 9
    3.1   Business 9
    3.2   Functional Design 9
    3.3   Development 10
    3.4   Environment Management 10
    3.5   Data Management 11
    3.6   Testing 11
    3.7   Recap 12

Chapter 4:   Software Testing Lifecycle 13
    4.1   STLC in SDLC 13
        4.1.1   Test Planning 14
        4.1.2   Test Preparation 14
        4.1.3   Test Execution 14
        4.1.4   Test Reporting 15
    4.2   Recap 15

Chapter 5: Test Planning ... 17
- 5.1 Contents of a Test Plan ... 17
- 5.2 Test Planning – Process Flow ... 19
- 5.3 Types of testing ... 20
  - 5.3.1 Static testing ... 20
  - 5.3.2 Dynamic Testing ... 20
  - 5.3.3 Black box testing ... 20
  - 5.3.4 White box testing ... 21
  - 5.3.5 Unit testing ... 21
  - 5.3.6 Integration testing ... 21
  - 5.3.7 Functional testing or System testing ... 21
  - 5.3.8 Regression testing ... 22
  - 5.3.9 User Acceptance testing ... 22
  - 5.3.10 Installation testing ... 22
  - 5.3.11 Security testing ... 23
  - 5.3.12 Browser Compatibility testing ... 23
- 5.4 Recap ... 23

Chapter 6: Test Preparation ... 24
- 6.1 Requirements analysis ... 25
  - 6.1.1 Validity ... 25
  - 6.1.2 Consistency ... 25
  - 6.1.3 Clarity ... 26
  - 6.1.4 Testability ... 26
- 6.2 Requirements Review and Traceability ... 26
  - 6.2.1 Business Requirements Document ... 26
  - 6.2.2 Functional Requirements Document ... 27
  - 6.2.3 Change Requests ... 27
  - 6.2.4 Use cases ... 28
- 6.3 What is Requirements Traceability? ... 28
  - 6.3.1 How to establish Traceability? ... 29
  - 6.3.2 Requirements Traceability Matrix ... 29
- 6.4 Creation of Test Cases ... 29
- 6.5 Test cases Review ... 29
- 6.6 Test Data generation/creation ... 30
- 6.7 Test Environment Readiness verification ... 30
- 6.8 Test Deliverables ... 31
- 6.9 Recap ... 31

Chapter 7: All about Test Cases/ Test Scripts ... 33
- 7.1 Definition ... 33

7.2	How to write a test case	33
7.2.1	Test Case examples	34
7.2.2	Positive Scenarios	39
7.2.3	Negative Scenarios	39
7.2.4	Inputs	40
7.3	Attributes of a Good Test case / Test Script	41
7.3.1	Detailed	41
7.3.2	Understandable	41
7.3.3	Controllable	41
7.3.4	Repeatable	41
7.3.5	Measureable	42
7.3.6	Successful	42
7.4	Contents of a Test case	42
7.4.1	A Sample Test Case Template	44
7.5	Tips to create high quality Test Cases	45
7.6	Recap	46
Chapter 8:	**All about Test Data**	**47**
8.1	What is Test Data?	47
8.2	Why is it important?	47
8.2.1	Valid Data	48
8.2.2	Invalid Data	48
8.2.3	Special Data	48
8.3	Test Data Optimization Techniques	49
8.3.1	Equivalence Partitioning	49
8.3.2	Boundary value Analysis	50
8.3.2	Decision Table or Decision Tree	50
8.4	Test Data Management Process	51
8.4.1	Test Data Requirements	52
8.4.2	Test Data Collation	52
8.4.3	Test Data Conditioning	53
8.4.4	Test Data Masking	53
8.4.5	Test Data Mapping	53
8.5	Recap	54
Chapter 9:	**Test Scripts Review**	**55**
9.1	Potential Hazards of Inadequate Test Cases Review	55
9.2	Purpose of Test Cases Review	56
9.3	Test Preparation Phase - Focus Areas during Review	56
9.4	Review Responsibilities	58
9.5	Test Execution Phase – Focus Areas During Review	58

9.6	Checklists and Review Reports	60
9.7	Most Common Errors Identified During Review	60
9.7.1	Coverage and Adequacy	60
9.7.2	Test Data Related	61
9.7.3	Correctness and Completeness	61
9.7.4	Documentation Errors	62
9.8	Key Benefits of Test Scripts Review	62
9.9	Recap	63

Chapter 10: Test Execution 64

10.1	Test Execution Strategy / Plan	64
10.1.1	Number or Test Passes or Test Runs	64
10.1.2	Script Status Tracking	65
10.1.3	Detailed Test Execution Plan	65
10.2	Test Execution – Entry Criteria	66
10.3	Test Execution – Exit Criteria	66
10.4	Recap	67

Chapter 11: Defects Management 68

11.1	What is a Defect Report?	68
11.2	How to write a good Defect Report?	69
11.3	Contents of a Defect Report	70
11.4	Defects Classification	71
11.4.1	Very High Severity/Show Stoppers	71
11.4.2	High Severity	71
11.4.3	Medium Severity	72
11.4.4	Low Severity	72
11.5	Defects Management Tools	72
11.6	Defects Tracking Process	73
11.6.1	Flow 1: Logged and Fixed	73
11.6.2	Flow 2: Logged and Fixed on second attempt	73
11.6.3	Flow 3: Logged and Document updated	74
11.6.4	Flow 4: Logged and Closed as invalid	74
11.7	Recap	75

Chapter 12: The Art of Error Guessing 76

12.1	Requirements Analysis	76
12.1.1	Scope Analysis - Too Many Changes?	76
12.2	Developer Analysis	77
12.2.1	Explicit Requirement is my Bible	77
12.2.2	Content is minor	78
12.2.3	One at a time approach	78

	12.2.4	Look and Feel – not my department!	78
12.3		Situation Analysis	79
12.4		Recap	79

Chapter 13: Test Reporting 80
   13.1   Test Status Reports 80
   13.2   Test Metrics 80
        13.2.1   Test Preparation Metrics 81
        13.2.2   Test Execution Metrics 81
        13.2.3   Defect Metrics 81
        13.2.4   Calculated Metrics 82
   13.3   Recap 84

Chapter 14: Key Levers to be a successful Tester 85
   14.1   Adopt a methodical approach to Testing 85
   14.2   Ensure Schedule / Effort Adherence 86
   14.3   Acquire the Business Knowledge 86
   14.4   Maintain high Quality Documentation 87
   14.5   Adopt Just in Time Status Reporting 87
   14.6   Track Issues to closure 88
   14.7   Hone-up the Technical Skill Levels 88
   14.8   Improve Communication and interaction 88
   14.9   Develop a keen eye for details 89
   14.10 Be Proactive 89

Chapter 15: Tips to Write Effective Tests for GUI Objects 90
   15.2   Text Box 90
        15.2.1   Text Box - Date Field 90
        15.2.2   Text Box - Numeric Field 91
   15.3   Radio Buttons 91
   15.4   Check Boxes 92
   15.5   Dropdown Menu 92
   15.6   List Box 93
   15.7   Command or Action Button 93

Chapter 16: Exercises 94
   16.1   Requirements Analysis Exercises 94
        16.1.1   Analyze the requirement and identify the gaps 94
        16.1.2   Analyze the requirement and comment on its validity 95
        16.1.3   Analyze the requirement and comment on its clarity 95
   16.2   Test Script Creation Exercises 96
   16.3   Test Data Optimization Exercises 96
   16.4   Defect Logging Exercises 97

Chapter 1: Introduction

This is the Information age. Information Technology is the most powerful break thru for everyone from all walks of life. IT has transformed the way we do business, the way we run the Government and even changed the way we teach our children.

Information Technology predominantly uses computer-based information systems to convert, store, protect, process, transmit and retrieve information. When these systems are built it is very important to ensure that they function properly and deliver the intended results.

Over the years, several techniques have been developed to help in the process of test case writing. Though the science behind this is still evolving, these techniques have been time tested and are proven to be effective. Any aspiring tester would be able to perform well by understanding these techniques/processes and utilizing them appropriately.

But then there is also the art of test case writing that one should be cognizant of – while following the techniques, the testers should also be able to get a little creative and create more successful tests by doing thorough analysis of the system under test and various other factors impacting the testing. In this book, the science behind test case writing is explained with the description, steps to create test cases, techniques to be used, and tips to test the UI objects. The art behind test case writing should be evolved by the tester and guidelines on how to successfully master the art are also provided in this book to trigger the thought process.

1.1   Who can become a Software Tester?

Any individual with the basic understanding of the computers with an aptitude to learn can become a Software Tester. While this is the basic requirement, to become a good Test Analyst one should have a thorough understanding of the Testing Concepts, Processes, Techniques, Tools, Methodologies and Best Practices. This book explains in detail the above basic aspects of Software Testing.

1.2   What is Software Testing?

Given below are some of the text book definitions for Software Testing:

Software Testing is the process of executing a program with the intent of finding errors Testing involves operation of a system or application and evaluating the results to ensure that they are consistent with the requirements.

Software testing is the process used to assess the quality of Computer applications

In order to understand the true definition of the term, we need to look closely at some of the terms used in the above definitions:

1.2.1 Quality of Software

Software quality is an indicator of how well the system is designed and implemented. From the end user perspective it is an indicator of whether the system is fit for use.

From the business perspective it indicates whether the system is compliant to the requirements.

1.2.3 Requirements

Requirement is the description of what the system is supposed to do and the functions that it is expected to deliver. This will include the content, Input and Output processing, User Interface, Reporting functions etc. Example: Calculator Application should have the ability to add, subtract, multiply and divide any two given whole numbers.

1.2.4 System/Application

Applications are systems typically built using the capabilities of a computer to perform the tasks of Information sharing and processing. Typically these applications have a User Interface making it easier for the user to learn and use the application. Examples of Computer applications: Word Processor, Calculator, Web site etc.

1.2.5 Errors

In software engineering, the term error refers to an incorrect action or calculation performed by software. It is the result of the code not being implemented correctly to deliver the functions defined in the requirements. It indicates that the system is either performing an undesired action or has failed to perform a desired action. Examples: Calculation errors, Input validation errors, Content display errors.

Software Testing is usually done to detect the defects and estimate the reliability of the system. In order to successfully accomplish this, Testing is not just an ad hoc attempt to execute the program - it encompasses the entire gamut of activities including Planning, Preparation, Execution, Reporting and Defects Management.

1.3 Recap

- Software Testing is the process of assessing the quality of Software applications to confirm that they are fit to use and are compliant with the requirements
- It holds a promising career for those who have the basic understanding of computers and have willingness to learn
- It is an important phase in the Software Development Life Cycle that requires proper planning and preparation
- A Requirement is the description of the functions that an application is expected to deliver
- Error/Defect indicates that the system is performing an undesired action or is not performing a desired action

Chapter 2: All about Systems

Testers should have the basic understanding of the application architecture to be able to analyze the impact of changes made to the different sub systems. Typically, applications will have multiple subsystems that interact with each other, a front end, a back end and possibly a host of mid-tier applications. Let's look at what each of these terms mean.

2.1 Front End

This is the Graphical User Interface that presents information to the users, collects inputs in various forms from the user, processes the information and passes back the relevant data to the back-end for further processing or future retrieval.

2.2 Mid – Tier

A Mid-Tier application is an intermediate program that mediates between the front-end and back-end systems.

2.3 Back End

A back-end application or program serves indirectly in support of the front-end services, by communicating with the required resource. The back-end application may interact directly with the front-end or via a mid-tier application. Most back ends are organized as database systems that store and process the data acquired from various front ends and send information back when requests are made by other systems.

2.4 What is a database?

A **data base** is a structured collection of records or data. Database Management System is the software used to organize and maintain the database. The software structure can e based on different database models. The model in most common use today is the relational model.

2.4.1 Relational Database Management System

RDBMS is a DBMS in which data is stored in the form of tables and the relationship among the data is also stored in the form of tables. Some of the top vendors of RDBMS products are Oracle, IBM, Microsoft, and Sybase.

2.4.1.1 Tables

A table is a set of data elements organized in columns and rows. For example, one table can be created to store customer information, one for Product information and one for order information for a database hosting the data for an order processing system.

2.4.1.2 Fields

A field is the basic unit of data in a record. For example, the typical fields in the Customer table would be Customer ID, First Name, Last Name, Address, City, State etc.

2.4.1.3 Records

A record is a set of fields – each field containing data pertaining to a unique entity. For example, in the customer table the data in the fields above pertaining to one customer is a record.

This is a very basic introduction to the database concepts. More in-depth reading is recommended in order to acquire database testing skills.

2.4.1.4 Database Query

Structured Query Language (SQL) is used to retrieve data from the databases. SQL queries can be written to retrieve data from one or more tables.

2.5 Recap

- A Front End is the Graphical User Interface (GUI) that presents information to the users and collects input in various forms from the user
- A **data base** is a structured collection of records or data. Database management systems are the software used to organize and maintain the database

- A table is a set of data elements organized in columns and rows
- A field is the basic unit of data in a record
- A record is a set of fields

Chapter 3: Know the Players - SDLC Stakeholders

To be able to work in a software organization, one should be familiar with the various stakeholders involved in Software development lifecycle. Each organization may have different naming conventions and levels under each group but a high level description of the stakeholder groups is provided below.

3.1 Business

This is the group that determines what should be included in the software that is being built. The Business Analysts determine what is required based on their knowledge of the domain, pulse of the market, legal requirements etc. Typically, they define the Business requirements – which essentially call out the functions that an end user should be able to perform on the software and list the actions that should not be allowed from a business perspective.

3.2 Functional Design

This group typically comprises of a bunch of Systems Analysts who understand both the technical and business sides well enough to create the Business/Technical Requirements. They basically translate the business requirements into a more detailed and technically viable design. The documents that they create are Business/technical Requirements, Business Rules, Wireframes, Use Cases and many more that explain in detail what should be built into the software and how different pieces of the software puzzle fit together. Test team should reach out to the SA team to clarify any questions regarding requirements and address any ambiguities in the documentation.

3.3 Development

Development team creates the actual software by building all the pieces and by putting them together. They create the detailed technical designs to determine how different sub systems will interact with each other and deliver the intended requirements. They build the application software according to the requirements. They perform Unit testing on individual components and also perform Assembly/Integration testing after they are put together before deploying to the test environment. They are also responsible for fixing any defects/issues identified by the testing team and delivering the updated application for retest and support the cyclical process until all significant defects are fixed and tested successfully. Test team will need to interact with the development team to clarify the defects reported, help recreate the defects and work closely to track issues to closure.

3.4 Environment Management

Some organizations have the development teams manage the test environment. Other bigger organizations have a separate group managing the different environments. This team is responsible for deploying the code in Test environments and ensuring that the environments remain stable during the testing timeframe. Test team will need to interact with this team if the test environments are not available for testing or if any issues are encountered by providing the details regarding the issues until a resolution is available.

3.5 Data Management

Test Data is a key requirement for the testing teams to exercise all the positive and negative test scenarios on the system. It is important to be able to set up the right kind of data needed for testing various real life scenarios. Some organizations provide the test teams the ability to tweak the data in the test environment while some bigger organizations have a dedicated team that manages the data requirements of various teams in order to have centralized control over the changes made to the data in the test environments. Test teams will need to work with the data teams to explain the data requirements, validate the data provided and get back to them if any discrepancies are observed in the test data provided.

3.6 Testing

Since our focus here is to understand the testing organization better, I saved the best for the last! This is the group that performs the critical function of exercising the software comprehensively in order to ensure that the defects in the software are identified and fixed before it is released to the end users. There may be different roles within this group but at a high level this team is responsible for test estimation, test planning, test preparation including scripts creation, test data identification, test environment validation, test execution, defects reporting, metrics collation and test closure.

3.7 Recap

Key stakeholders are:

1. Business
2. Functional Design
3. Development
4. Environment Management
5. Data Management
6. Testing

Chapter 4: Software Testing Lifecycle

Software Testing Lifecycle (STLC) is a significant subset of the Software Development Lifecycle (SDLC). It encompasses Planning, preparation, execution phases of testing.

4.1 STLC in SDLC

Figure 4.1

4.1.1 Test Planning

Test Planning starts when the requirements for the software are finalized by the business and technical teams. The test planning team analyzes the extent of testing needed and estimates the effort/resource requirements as a first step.

As soon as the basic details are gathered, a Test Plan should be prepared for every Software testing project undertaken. A robust Test plan should include in explicit detail the scope, test strategy, schedule, resources, tools and templates. The plan should also identify the key risks and dependencies that may impact testing.

4.1.2 Test Preparation

Test Preparation phase includes the activities that are needed to get geared into performing the test execution when the software is ready for test. Typically test preparation starts right after the initial test planning is completed and includes Requirements analysis, Test cases or scripts creation, Review, Test data gathering and Verification of Test environment.

4.1.3 Test Execution

Test Execution phase begins when the software is delivered in the test environment. It entails running the test cases/scripts by performing various actions on the software and verifying whether the results observed are matching the requirements definitions. If the results match – the test passes and if there are discrepancies in the results – the test fails. For every failed test, a defect report is created and the development team is notified to fix the problem. Once the defect fix is delivered in the test environment the test is run again and this process repeats until all the tests pass. There could be exceptions to this rule – the details shall be discussed in the chapter on Test Execution. Defect Management is an important aspect during the test execution phase and the details can be found in a later chapter.

4.1.4 Test Reporting

It is important to define a detailed status reporting process during each phase of Testing in order to keep all the stakeholders updated about the progress, identify the bottlenecks and issues hampering test activities. Reports should be delivered daily or weekly based on the needs of the project and the details of the report should be altered based on the recipients of the report.

The report should clearly provide summary updates on % completion, % pending, issues and risks followed by the details as needed. Determining the right amount of details/metrics is the key to create a meaningful status report.

4.2 Recap

Software Testing is an integral part of Software Development lifecycle and includes the following important phases.

- Software Testing lifecycle (STLC encompasses Planning, preparation, execution phases of testing.
- Test Planning starts when the requirements for the software are finalized by the business and technical teams.
- Test Preparation phase includes the activities that are needed to get geared into performing the test execution
- It is important to define a detailed status reporting process during each phase of Testing in order to keep all the stakeholders updated about the progress, identify the bottlenecks and issues hampering test activities

Chapter 5: Test Planning

Failing to plan is planning to fail. Software Testing is all about setting a product up for success. Hence proper planning of the testing activities is very important and essential. A Test Plan should be prepared for every Software testing project undertaken. A robust Test plan should include in explicit detail the scope, test strategy, schedule, resources, tools and templates. The plan should also identify the key risks and dependencies that may impact testing.

5.1 Contents of a Test Plan

A good test plan should contain the relevant details about the project to enable the execution of the testing activities based on the project needs and schedule. Each organization will have a template for all deliverables including Test Plan. The typical contents of a test plan are listed below.

1. Project Name
2. Application under test
3. Author Name
4. Revision history of document including authors, dates, approvals
5. Table of Content
6. Purpose of document and intended audience
7. Testing Scope
8. Document References - Requirements, Design documents
9. Test Strategy and Types of testing

10. Test Schedule and Key Milestones
11. Testing Process
12. Test Data management process
13. Defect Management Process
14. Test Phase Entry/Exit Criteria
15. Test Suspension/Resumption criteria
16. Test Deliverables
17. Test Organization Chart
18. Roles and Responsibilities
19. Assumptions and dependencies
20. Risk Management Process
21. Test Environment Requirements
22. Test Environment setup and configuration Plan
23. Tools and Licensing needs
24. Test Automation Strategy, if applicable
25. Status Reporting and Meetings
26. Test Metrics
27. Training needs and Plan
28. Escalation Process
29. Test Closure Process
30. Glossary

5.2 Test Planning – Process Flow

Test Lead owns the creation of test plan by collating the relevant information needed to cover all aspects of testing to deliver the project within the schedule. Once the plan is created, it should be reviewed with the Test owner/manager, changes to be made based on the feedback and get approval. The base lined test plan should be shared with everyone on the testing team in order to understand the plan and their tasks according to the plan.

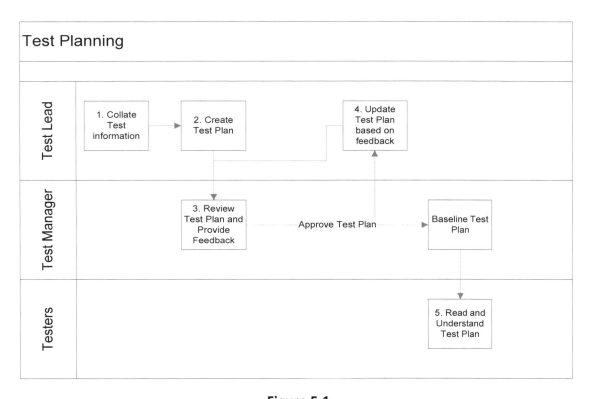

Figure 5.1

Many projects also create a detailed task level test plan to track assignment of work and progress. This may be done using Microsoft Project Plan or other planning tools.

A separate book can be written on Test planning as it is a very important phase within the testing lifecycle but the testers should have the high level knowledge of what happens in the planning phase and also provide any inputs to the plan if they identify any issues with the plan from practical implementation perspective.

5.3 Types of testing

5.3.1 Static testing

Static testing involves verification of documents to identify any potential errors in the documents like functional design or requirements. The purpose of this test is to catch any errors earlier in the lifecycle – so this type of testing is typically completed prior to test execution phase.

5.3.2 Dynamic Testing

Dynamic testing refers to the testing that is performed on the application under test after the code and/or the changes are implemented.

5.3.3 Black box testing

Black box testing is based on requirements and functionality. It is called black box because the Testing team will not have any exposure to technical design or code.

5.3.4 White box testing

White box testing is based on coverage of code statements, branches, paths, conditions. It is called white box or sometimes Glass box testing because this type of testing is typically done by the developers that have the visibility and knowledge of the technical design and logic the code.

5.3.5 Unit testing

Unit testing covers just one unit for test – a specific function or page or code module. This type of testing is typically done by the developers that have the visibility and knowledge of the technical design and logic the code.

5.3.6 Integration testing

Integration testing covers testing of two or more units to validate their interactions – a specific function or page or code module or applications. This type of testing is typically done by the developers that have the visibility and knowledge of the technical design and logic the code.

5.3.7 Functional testing or System testing

Functional testing refers to the Black-box testing based on requirements and functionality. This covers the system as a whole.

5.3.8 Regression testing

Regression testing refers to the retest of functions after defect fixes or changes are made to the system to ensure that the fix/change has not impacted the functions that were tested successfully before. Regression should be planned to be done towards the end of the test execution phase providing for defect fix turnaround time before the testing cycle ends.

5.3.9 User Acceptance testing

User Acceptance testing is done by the system analyst group or business users who are very close to the end users to validate that the system conforms to the requirements. This is the last phase of testing before the system is rolled out to the end users. Use cases are typically written like stories depicting an end user situation identifying the actors to run thru the scenarios.

5.3.10 Installation testing

Installation testing refers to testing of the install/uninstall processes to ensure that the end user is able to install the system without issues in case of stand-alone applications.

5.3.11   Security testing

Security testing refers to verification of the controls that are created to prevent unauthorized access to the system, protection of sensitive information etc. Specialized skills may be needed to perform this type of testing.

5.3.12   Browser Compatibility testing

Browser Compatibility Testing refers to validating the performance of the system across various browser/operating system combinations and different browser versions and OS versions.

5.4   Recap

- Test Planning is an important phase in testing lifecycle
- A comprehensive test plan is a pivotal deliverable for a testing project
- Plan should be reviewed by all the testers though these are typically created by the test leads
- There various types of testing that a tester should be aware of in order to plan testing efforts based on the type of testing.

Chapter 6: Test Preparation

Test Preparation phase includes the activities that are needed to get geared into performing the test execution when the software is ready for test. Typically test preparation starts right after initial test planning is completed and includes Requirements analysis, Test cases creation, Review, Test data gathering and Verification of Test environment.

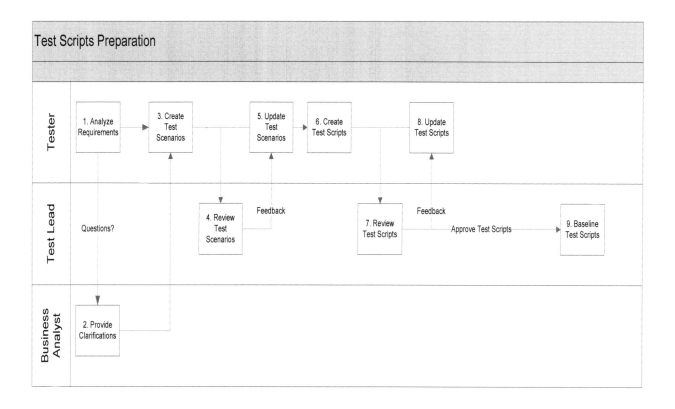

Figure 6.1

6.1 Requirements analysis

Software requirement is a descriptions of the features that should be included as part of the application. There could be different levels of detail included in the requirements based on the stage in which it is created. But specific details of what exactly should be seen on the system should be called out in the requirements.

Thorough analysis of the requirements is a pre-requisite for test cases creation. The tester should understand the requirements definition clearly and be able to translate the requirements into positive and negative test cases. The requirements should be analyzed with the focus on the following criteria.

6.1.1 Validity

Requirements should be valid and applicable to the application under test and the business rules that govern the application. Any requirement that is incorrectly defined should be re-defined.

6.1.2 Consistency

Requirements defined for an application should be consistent while defining the features and functions for the application. Any contradictions between requirements should be clarified to ensure that there is consistency in the requirements definition across all application functionalities.

6.1.3 Clarity

Any ambiguous statements should be questioned and clarification should be sought. A tester should never make assumptions based on vague requirements.

6.1.4 Testability

The requirements should be validated from a testability perspective. Even a well-defined requirement that cannot be tested needs to be revisited.

6.2 Requirements Review and Traceability

A Tester should have a very good understanding of the inputs into testing, testing process, Testing techniques, Tools, Templates and reports or outputs from testing activities. This chapter briefly explains the various input documents that are pertinent for a tester in order to be able to test the system.

6.2.1 Business Requirements Document

Business Requirements document contains detailed specifications of the new features or changes that the Business requires to be introduced in the System. This document will provide insight into the purpose of the changes to the system and the expected outcome from a Business perspective.

Authors: Business Analysts

Approvers: Business Sponsors

Audience: Developers, Testers, Business users

6.2.2 Functional Requirements Document

Functional Design Documents provide specific details on the changes to the system behavior in order to meet the Business requirements. This will include multiple functions that are impacted by the change and the business rules around these functions. Functional design documents will include the User Interface details, the action triggers (For example, "clicking on Ok button"), different scenarios for triggering the action, business rules for each of the triggers and may also include the data dictionary, navigation rules etc. for the application.

Authors: Business Analysts
Approvers: Business Sponsors
Audience: Developers, Testers, Business users

6.2.3 Change Requests

Any change that is made to the Business Requirements resulting in a change to the system after the Business Requirements are finalized, shall be typically processed as a Change Request. This will also contain specifications of the changes to be made to the system. Any change request will undergo a review and approval process before it is implemented.

Authors: Business Analysts
Approvers: Change Control Board

Audience: Developers, Testers, Business users

6.2.4 Use cases

Use cases describe the interaction between the end user and the system while performing a series of actions in order to test that the behavior of the system is in conformance with the Functional Requirements. Use cases are typically prepared as tools for carrying out User Acceptance testing.

Authors: Business Analysts
Approvers: Business sponsors
Audience: Developers, Testers, Business users

6.3 What is Requirements Traceability?

Software Requirements define the features that should be built or implemented as part of the software system. In order to confirm that the system has been built according to the specifications, it is imperative to ensure that the implementation of the requirements is tracked properly. Mapping the requirements to the design, code and test scripts enables to confirm that the requirement has been taken into account while designing, coding and testing the system. This is referred to as Requirements Traceability – the ability to trace a requirement to design, code and test scripts.

6.3.1 How to establish Traceability?

Requirements Traceability is established by creating a mapping of design document, code segment and test script with each requirement.

6.3.2 Requirements Traceability Matrix

Requirements Traceability Matrix is a tool that helps in establishing the mapping to the Requirement specifications and tracking the various work products created during the Software development lifecycle.

6.4 Creation of Test Cases

Test cases are the most important tools in a tester's toolkit. Successful test cases should be written in a manner to verify that the application under test is working as designed and also to ensure that it is not yielding any undesired results. The tester should wear the end-user hat while identifying the test cases and create scripts using the requirement documents and technical design documents as base inputs. Test case design techniques should be adopted to ensure adequate test coverage for each requirement. These are elaborated in the following chapter.

6.5 Test cases Review

It is common for the creator/author to overlook the faults of the work products as familiarity breeds error immunity. Hence it is important to define and plan for multiple reviews for test cases. Lack of proper review of test cases could cause defects to creep into production. The principal goal of Software testing is to minimize defect seepage into production and fixing an erroneous test case early in the life cycle is a required step in that direction.

6.6 Test Data generation/creation

Test data is the input data that a tester uses while testing a software application. It could be the username/password of a specific type of user, it could be different combinations of input data for testing a specific data entry field, it could be valid or invalid. Valid test data would result in the system returning expected results and invalid test data would result in invoking the error handling mechanism built into the application.

A data entry field can be tested using various combinations of valid and invalid test data and it could result in an enormous amount of test data and thereby increase the number of scripts to be executed to very high proportions. Hence it is important to apply time tested test data definition techniques for this exercise. Identifying the right kind of data for testing is the backbone of a successful test effort.

6.7 Test Environment Readiness verification

Test environment that simulates the production environment closely is a pre-requisite for successful testing. The test environment encompasses the front end, middle tier and back ends applications/tools. It is important to ensure that the access to the test environments is established well ahead of the test execution schedule, ensure that the required data is loaded onto the test database.

6.8 Test Deliverables

The important deliverables from the testing team a tester should know about are listed below.

- Test Plan
- Test Strategy
- Test data requirement document
- Test Scripts
- Test Scripts Review checklists
- Test Execution Plan
- Requirements Traceability Matrix
- Defect Reports
- Test Results Summary
- Status Reports

6.9 Recap

The key activities in Test Preparation Phase are listed below.

- Thorough analysis of the requirements is a pre-requisite for test cases creation
- Requirements Traceability refers to mapping of the requirements to the design, code and test scripts

- Test cases are the most important tools in a tester's toolkit. Successful test cases should be written in a manner to verify that the application under test is working as designed and also to ensure that it is not yielding any undesired results. Test Cases/Scripts Review
- Test Data generation/creation is an important phase in STLC. . Valid test data would result in the system returning expected results and invalid test data would result in invoking the error handling mechanism built into the application.
- It is important to ensure that the access to the test environments is established well ahead of the test execution schedule

Chapter 7: All about Test Cases/ Test Scripts

This chapter will provide you with all the ammunition required to write effective test cases.

7.1 Definition

A test script or a test case is a tool that is used to test individual features/functionalities of the system under test which comprises of the steps that need to be executed on the system and the expected results from the system. A good test case will specify the actions to be performed along with expected result for each action separately and clearly.

Though the terms Test Script and Test Case are often times used interchangeably, Test Case typically refers to the description of the tests that are run manually and Test Script refers to the tests created using a test automation tool.

7.2 How to write a test case

Test cases or scripts should be written to exercise a function or feature on the application under test thoroughly to identify any errors or defects in the system. The tests created should target to verify that each and every requirement for the system is tested for the positive and negative scenarios.

Well, this high level description on how to write the test case could be overwhelming to a novice tester. So this is elaborated further with an example. In the lighter vein, let's assume that there is a requirement to put a Hippopotamus inside the refrigerator (I have seen the Elephant example used before – so choosing a Hippo here instead!). The first step would be to understand the requirement. This requirement can be dissected into the below details.

- **Requirement:** Put a Hippopotamus inside a refrigerator
- **System:** In this case, the system under test is the refrigerator
- **Input:** Hippopotamus
- **Expected Result:** Hippo should go inside the refrigerator

7.2.1 Test Case examples

To test the above requirement, the test case needs to be written to validate that a hippo can be put inside the refrigerator. Here is an example of a test case.

Steps	Results
Validate that a Hippo can be put inside the refrigerator	Hippo should go into the refrigerator

Table 7.1

Take a minute and review the test case and think about whether this will be effective in testing the requirement thoroughly and identify defects in the system? If you have your tester's hat on, you would recognize that this is not an effective test.

How could you translate this requirement into effective test cases?

The next step would be to analyze the requirement and identify any flaws or lack of detail in the requirement and get clarifications from the author of the requirement document. DO NOT assume anything.

Some questions that would need to be asked in this case would be:

1. What are the size specifications for the Refrigerator and the Hippo?
2. Will the Refrigerator accommodate all sizes of Hippos? If not, what are the size ranges that would fit in?
3. What happens if the Hippo is too big for the Refrigerator and does not go in?
4. If the Hippo is in and the door doesn't close, what happens? Is closing of the door mandatory?

Now let's assume that the above questions are clarified with the below answers.

1. Refrigerator is large and Hippos come in different sizes
2. Refrigerator will hold a small or a medium or a large Hippo
3. If the Hippo doesn't go in, an error should be triggered to say "Hippo is too big for the refrigerator. Please try again with a small or a medium or a large Hippo"

4. If the refrigerator doesn't close after putting the Hippo in, an error should be triggered to say "Hippo is too big for the refrigerator. Please try again with a small or a medium or a large Hippo"
5. Only one Hippo can be put inside the Refrigerator at a time. If more than one Hippo is put in, an error should be triggered to say " Only one Hippo at a time".

Let's attempt writing test cases for the above requirement with the clarifications received.

Pre-Requisites for the test:

1. Get a Large size refrigerator
2. Get Hippos in various sizes – Small, Medium, Large, Extra large

#	Test Case Description	Steps	Expected Results	Pass / Fail
1	Validate that a small Hippo can be put in the Large Refrigerator	1. Bring a Small Hippo near the Refrigerator 2. Open the Refrigerator door 3. Put the Small Hippo inside the Refrigerator 4. Close the refrigerator door	The small Hippo should go inside the refrigerator and the door should close all the way.	

#	Test Case Description	Steps	Expected Results	Pass / Fail
2	Validate that a Medium Hippo can be put in the Large Refrigerator	1. Bring a Medium Hippo near the Refrigerator 2. Open the Refrigerator door 3. Put the Medium Hippo inside the Refrigerator 4. Close the refrigerator door	The Medium Hippo should go inside the refrigerator and the door should close all the way.	
3	Validate that a Large Hippo can be put in the Large Refrigerator	1. Bring a Large Hippo near the Refrigerator 2. Open the Refrigerator door 3. Put the Large Hippo inside the Refrigerator 4. Close the refrigerator door	The Large Hippo should go inside the refrigerator and the door should close all the way.	

#	Test Case Description	Steps	Expected Results	Pass / Fail
4	Validate that an error is triggered when an Extra Large Hippo is put in the Large Refrigerator	1. Bring an Extra Large Hippo near the Refrigerator 2. Open the Refrigerator door 3. Put the Extra Large Hippo inside the Refrigerator	The below error should be triggered. "Hippo is too big for the refrigerator. Please try again with a small or a medium or a large Hippo"	
5	Validate that an error is triggered when more than one Hippo is put in the Large Refrigerator	1. Bring a small and a medium Hippo near the Refrigerator 2. Open the Refrigerator door 3. Put both the Hippos inside the Refrigerator	The below error should be triggered. " Only one Hippo at a time, please"	

Table 7.2

The above set of test cases contains positive and negative scenarios to test the requirement thoroughly to confirm that the system meets the requirement.

7.2.2 Positive Scenarios

The tests that confirm that the requirements defined are implemented correctly. In this case, the requirement is to put small/medium/large size Hippos into a large refrigerator. So, the tests 1, 2 and 3 cover the positive scenarios that confirm that the requirements are met or not.

7.2.3 Negative Scenarios

The tests that confirm that if any assumptions change and unexpected inputs are provided or unexpected actions are performed, the system is able to handle those situations without breaking. In the above example, tests 4 and 5 are the negative scenarios where abnormal input is used and the system reaction is validated.

The focus of the testers should be to cover all possible negative scenarios even if they are not explicitly called out in the requirements in order to confirm that the system is able to gracefully handle abnormal inputs without breaking.

Why is the validation of negative scenarios important? Typically, the focus of Software code is more on error handling than on the implementation of the requirement/function.

For example, consider an "If, Else" statement – there will be a couple of lines of code in the "If" statement covering the positive scenario that will include entry of valid information or performing an expected action on the system under test but there may be a number of "Else" statements within the code, to cover the negative scenarios or error scenarios that handle the errors with a user friendly statement being presented to the user. Because of this, it is important for the tester to put on the developers hat to think through and confirm that all possible error handling has been covered adequately and that the system does not break if any unexpected action is performed or abnormal values are entered by the user.

7.2.4 Inputs

Inputs in this case are the different sizes or Hippos. Inputs selected in the tests should include not only the explicit items called out in the requirement but also the implicit items. In our example, there were multiple implicit requirements (extra-large will not fit, only one Hippo at a time that were clarified later). For every system testing with different input types will be very important to ensure that results yielded for different categories of input are as per the requirements.

Now, read the explanation on how to write test cases given at the start of this section again and ponder for a minute.

Test cases or scripts should be written to exercise a function or feature on the application under test thoroughly to identify any errors or defects in the system. The tests created should target to verify that each and every requirement for the system is tested for the positive and negative scenarios. Hopefully, it should make more sense now!

7.3 Attributes of a Good Test case / Test Script

7.3.1 Detailed

A test script should be very detailed in describing the actions to be performed on the system step by step and corresponding expected results. It should contain all the information needed for someone who is not familiar with the system to also be able to run the tests using the test script.

7.3.2 Understandable

It is recommended that the scripts are written clearly without any ambiguity. Use of any jargons or abbreviations should be avoided. Simple terms should be used to capture the actions to be performed and responses from the system.

7.3.3 Controllable

The test scripts should have pre-defined inputs that are controllable. For example, the size of the Hippos are finite and pre-defined – Small, Large etc.

7.3.4 Repeatable

The scripts should be written in such a way that the same script can be used repeatedly whenever the script needs to be run.

7.3.5 Measureable

The results should be captured as measurable – to indicate whether the script was executed successfully or not.

7.3.6 Successful

A good test script should identify the possible errors in the system so that they can be addressed in a timely manner. This is why it is very important to think thru all the positive and negative scenarios and include various input categories in the tests to exercise the functionality completely.

7.4   Contents of a Test case

Templates for test cases/scripts may differ for different projects based on the unique needs but typically a good test case/script should contain the below attributes.

- Project Name
- Function Name
- Author
- Date Prepared
- Reviewer
- Date Reviewed
- Pre-requisites/Set up procedures
- Test scenario

- Actions/Steps
- Expected Result
- Actual Result
- Date Executed
- Pass/Fail
- Defect # (for failed scripts)

7.4.1 A Sample Test Case Template

Project Name: Function/Feature Name:

Author: Date Prepared:

Reviewer: Date Reviewed:

Test Preparation Effort (in hours):   Review Effort (in hours):

Rework Effort (in hours):

Pre-requisites / Set up procedures:

#	Test Scenario	Actions / Steps	Expected Results	Test Data	Actual Results	Executed Date	Executed By	Pass / Fail	Defect #

Table 7.3

7.5 Tips to create high quality Test Cases

- Adopt/Create a template for test cases document and ensure that all the testers in the team use this template. Based on the needs of the project, items can be added to the template.

- Be aware of the importance of the test data gathering techniques like equivalence partitioning and Boundary Value analysis and apply these techniques while preparing the cases by emphasizing the importance of these techniques.

- Perform thorough requirements review with the aim of identifying the test scenarios – positive and negative, explicit and implicit, exceptional scenarios etc., before preparing the test cases

- Adopt the practice of writing the test cases in detail. Each action should be captured as a step and each response should be captured as Expected Result.

- Use definite statements in the Steps/Actions to be performed to test a condition and in the expected behavior. The dependencies or pre-requisites can be detailed separately.

- Inculcate the practice of constantly monitoring changes to the requirements in order to ensure that the test cases are updated as and when the requirements are changed.

- Understand the importance of writing test cases that are free from grammatical errors. Grammatical errors could even cause misinterpretation of sentences, in some instances besides being unaesthetic.

- Ensure that the actual results are documented while the tests are run. Also, document the defect details, retest details in the test case document.

7.6 Recap

- Test cases/Scripts are documents that describe action to be performed and
- expected results for each action in order to test a function on the system
- They should include positive and negative scenarios
- Test scripts should be detailed, repeatable, clear and successful in
- identifying the issues with the system under test
- A tester should follow the best practices while creating tests with the intent of identifying defects

Chapter 8: All about Test Data…

8.1 What is Test Data?

Test data is the set of input values used to test the response from the system for different combination of input values. If we call the entire range of input values for the function as Domain then a test data set is a subset of the domain used for testing to confirm that the system functions as per requirement for each category of the data domain. In the Hippo in the refrigerator example, the input values or the data will be size of the Hippo (Small, Medium, Large, and Extra Large). This becomes more complex when numeric input values need to be included in test and that is when data identification techniques should be used to select the optimal test data set. Test data could be referring to a single data attribute like for example, an email address or it could refer to a combination of attributes like, an order in Shipped status placed by a member belonging to a special category.

8.2 Why is it important?

Most of the software systems developed today, gather data and process information for various purposes. To test an order processing system, a host of combinations of data related to Customer attributes, Products, Order, Payment, Shipping, Order History etc. will need to be included in the tests. Each of these categories will have different combinations yielding different results from the system and hence it is important to understand what kind of data to use for testing and how to identify the most important data elements to include during testing. A comprehensive test data set would include valid data, invalid data, data reflecting the special properties of the data domain and special properties of the function implemented.

8.2.1 Valid Data

Test data set should include all the possible categories of valid input values to confirm that the system is processing them as expected. Valid data in the Hippo example are Small, Medium and Large Hippos.

8.2.2 Invalid Data

Test data set should also include all possible invalid input values to confirm that the system is handling the exceptions in a user friendly manner. Typically, a user-friendly error should be displayed if invalid input values are fed into the system. In the Hippo example, Extra Large and two hippos are invalid values that should generate an exception and trigger the user friendly error message.

8.2.3 Special Data

In some cases, specific data items within a valid data range can be treated uniquely. For example, a insurance company may have the valid age range as 1 – 100 and may have a special discount for members that are born in the year 2001 when the company was incorporated. In this case, members belonging to this category will need to be included specifically in the test.

8.3 Test Data Optimization Techniques

Several techniques could be applied to ensure that the optimal data set is identified for testing as exhaustive testing may not be possible for the data intensive tests. Using these test data optimization techniques, adequate coverage of tests can be ensured. A couple of frequently used techniques are elaborated below.

8.3.1 Equivalence Partitioning

Equivalence partitioning is identifying the various classes within the test data domain and ensuring that at least one representative data from each of the class is included in testing. The main assumption behind this is that all data elements belonging to a class will all share the same attributes and hence generate similar results.

Classes

- Negative values
- Acceptable values (any number between 1 and 100)
- Values greater than hundred

Out of Range Classes

- Zero (should be considered as a special value)
- Alpha value
- Special character

After classifying the input domain, adequate representative elements from each class should be included in the test data set.

8.3.2 Boundary value Analysis

Boundary value analysis calls for identifying the extremal values in a domain and ensuring that these values are included in the test data set. For example, if the input data range is 1-10, then the boundary values are 1 and 10.

Epsilon points are the values that are one up and one below the extremal points. In the above example, these will be 0,2,9 and 11.

While creating a test data set, a tester should ensure that equivalence partitioning is done and after doing that should also include the boundary values and epsilon points in the test data set. Usually doing these two things go hand-in-hand. You'll try to do boundary value analysis for each class identified and thus create the test data set to also include special values and values that are not in range.

8.3.2 Decision Table or Decision Tree

While dealing with data intensive test cases involving many parameters and combinations thereof, the focus of testing should be to ensure that all important combinations of the input parameters are included in the tests. This could be accomplished by using the Decision table of decision tree approach.

Creating a Decision table will require tabulating the input parameters and capturing the key inputs values for each of the parameters and validating this against the requirement to confirm that the coverage of tests is adequate. Let's go back to the hippo in the refrigerator example. The below decision table would capture the scenarios to test the requirement.

Hippo Size	Number of Hippos	Positive / Negative	Expected Result
Small	1	Positive	Should fit inside the Refrigerator
Medium	1	Positive	Should fit inside the Refrigerator
Large	1	Positive	Should fit inside the Refrigerator
Extra large	1	Negative	Error should be displayed
1 Small, 1 Medium	2	Negative	Error should be displayed

Table 8.1

This may seem pretty simple since the number of parameters is less in this case. But when it comes to optimizing the scenarios for multiple input parameters and the hundreds/thousands/ millions of data combinations thereof, this technique will be very handy.

8.4 Test Data Management Process

In order to ensure that appropriate and adequate data scenarios are used during the testing process, test data collation and usage should be managed systematically.

8.4.1 Test Data Requirements

For any testing project, the data requirements need to be identified as soon as the test scenarios are created. Sometimes if the tests are data intensive, test data needs will need to be identified even before test scenarios are written and may be used as the basis to create test scenarios.

This basically involves thorough review of requirements to come up with the list or combinations of all relevant data values that will need to be included in the tests in order to confirm that the system is able to correctly handle all the data permutations and combinations and does not break.

8.4.2 Test Data Collation

Test data collation can be a tedious effort and should not be undermined for bigger projects involving multiple systems and sub-systems and this should be carefully planned taking into consideration the inter-dependencies between the systems and data set up processes. In some cases, the data set up will need to be a sequential process and may be time consuming and such items will need to be planned upfront in the project to avoid any impact to the schedules.

Test data may be just any values entered by the testers which will be stored in the databases and retrieved later. Or it could be specific set of data identified from the databases. For example, to set up a new member any data could be entered. But to test whether a specific type of member is able to login to the application, the data meeting the test requirements will need to be queried from the database. More often than not, data needed is collated from the database systems where the test data is stored.

8.4.3 Test Data Conditioning

Once the required data is identified, further tweaking of data attributes may be needed based on the tests that need to be run. In order to do this, the testers will either have to work with the team that has access to the test databases or procure access to the databases in order make the necessary changes to the data. The process of updating the data attributes to suit the testing needs is referred to as test data conditioning.

8.4.4 Test Data Masking

Most test databases are typically loaded with the data from the real time production environment. There may be sensitive data stored in these databases that cannot be opened up for access to even the Information technology team due to privacy/data security concerns. Hence when such production data copy happens, the copied data is masked using complex algorithms to change the sensitive information like address, Date of birth, Credit Card Number, Social Security number etc. This process of updating the data attributes in order to protect the real time production data from being exposed to the technical team is called test data masking.

8.4.5 Test Data Mapping

Once the test data needs are identified and collated, it is important to map the data to the relevant test cases/scripts so that it can be readily available for the testers during test execution. Some organizations follow the practice of having a central test data repository and give reference to the data location within the test cases. Either way, the mapping between the data items and scripts should be established prior to test start date as part of the test preparation process.

8.5 Recap

- Test data is the set of input values used to test the response from the system for different combinations of input values
- Test data needs should be identified during the test preparation phase
- Test data optimization techniques should be utilized
- Data should be collated prior to test start date
- Test data conditioning should be done based on the test needs
- Test data should be mapped to the test cases/scripts

Chapter 9:   Test Scripts Review

Software Testing plays a vital role in ensuring the quality of a software product. Test cases are the key tools for testing. Hence review of test cases is very much pertinent in ensuring that they are correct, adequate and succeed in finding the obvious and latent defects in the Software. Many a times, testing time is shortened due to various reasons and hence test cases reviews are either overlooked or ad hoc reviews are done just as a formality. There have been many instances where no review or inadequate review of test cases has caused lots of production problems.

9.1   Potential Hazards of Inadequate Test Cases Review

Lack of proper review of test cases could cause defects to creep into production. Thus production problems could be reported which would not reflect well on the quality of the Software. The cost of fixing the defects at this stage would be substantially higher than what would have been the cost of fixing if it were identified during the testing phase.

Even if sporadic reviews are done without documenting the findings, the purpose will not be served. Ad hoc reviews will not help to identify the problem areas and improve the test case creation efficiency.

9.2 Purpose of Test Cases Review

Any work product that is considered as a deliverable, should be peer reviewed. Test cases are important deliverables for the testing team that fall under this category. The aim of test cases review should be to double check whether the intent and the content of the test cases are correctly documented.

It is very important to ensure that effective test cases are written that successfully unearth as many defects as possible during testing. Hence a check is required to appraise the test cases to verify the following aspects:

- Test cases are written with the intent to detect the defects
- Understanding of the requirements is correct
- Impact areas are identified and brought under test scope
- Test data set is correct and represents every possible class of the domain
- Positive and negative scenarios are covered
- Expected behavior is documented correctly
- Test coverage is adequate

9.3 Test Preparation Phase - Focus Areas during Review

During the Test preparation phase, after the test scenarios are identified and test conditions and cases are built for each scenario, a thorough and detailed review should be done. The focus of test review during this phase should be on the following areas.

1. Ensure that the correct template is used.
2. Verify that the basic information about the test cases document like the Description, Author name, Date prepared, Requirement Reference etc. have been filled in correctly.
3. Check whether the implicit and the explicit requirements have been converted into Test scenarios.
4. Ensure that the areas that could be possibly affected by the requirement under test are also tested to rule out possible breakage.
5. Validate the Test data set. Ensure that testing techniques like Equivalence Partitioning, Boundary Value analysis etc., are appropriately used. Check whether boundary values, invalid values and special values are included in the Test data set.
6. Ensure that all possible negative scenarios have been identified and included in the test scenarios.
7. Check whether the test data is properly embedded into the test cases.
8. Verify that the steps for each scenario have been given in proper sequence and that the steps state the user actions to be carried out in clear terms. The steps should be definite, specific and not generic. For example, "If", "In case" statements should be avoided.
9. Ensure that Expected Results contain the details of how the system should respond to the user action specified in the respective step.
10. Ensure that vague and ambiguous statements are not used in Steps or in the Expected behavior. For example, Vague statements like "Appropriate message/value/screen" etc, should not be part of expected result. Every detail should be clearly spelt out.

11. Ensure that separate test cases are written for verification of multiple behaviors of the application. Ensure that too many things are not included to be verified under one expected output.
12. Check if all statements are free from grammatical errors and typos.

9.4 Review Responsibilities

Test Managers should ensure that test cases review is a planned activity. During the planning phase, reviewers should be identified for preparation and execution phases and the time for such reviews should be factored into the estimates. Reviewers should be assigned based their expertise in the area under test. Peer reviews should be compulsory and reviews by leads/managers also should be done as an additional check.

The onus of getting the test cases reviewed should be on the author of the test case document and the author should make sure that the review comments are addressed appropriately by making the necessary updates in the test cases document.

The reviewer should make sure that all the focus areas are verified during the review. After providing the review comments, the reviewer should also ensure that the comments are closed and the necessary changes are made in the test cases document.

9.5 Test Execution Phase – Focus Areas During Review

During the test execution phase, doing a review after the cases are executed is very important though not many follow this process. At this stage, ensuring that the test cases have been actually run successfully and that the results have been documented clearly is vital. The focus of test cases review during this phase should be on the following areas.

1. Ensure that the execution details like executed by and executed date, been filled up correctly.
2. Check if all the test cases have been executed and the results are marked correctly. Verify that the defect details, actual results, retest details with the date have been included for the failed test cases. If a defect is not fixed, the reasons for the same or some disposition should be specified.
3. Ensure that the actual results are captured for each of the steps and for each re-run of the steps for the failed test cases.
4. Check if the reason for failure from testing perspective is identified wherever possible. For example, invalid input data, new functionality not tested before, existing problem etc.
5. Verify if a peer was able to recreate the defects that have been reported and that the details of such recreation have been recorded in the test cases document.
6. If the test cases have been executed in different environments (i.e. browsers, Operating systems etc.), then check if the results of such tests have been captured in separate columns.
7. Ensure that the metrics related to the test cases have been updated in all applicable metrics documents. (Number of test cases prepared, executed, Number of test case executions with defects, Total Number of defects etc.)
8. Check if all statements are free from grammatical errors and typos.

9.6 Checklists and Review Reports

Having identified the methodology to be adopted while reviewing the test cases, it would be prudent to come up with a checklist to be used based on the focus areas identified above and also including any other project specific checks. Sample checklists have been provided in the Appendix section.

In addition to this, the review reports should also be prepared – documenting and categorizing the issues identified during reviews, so that the testing process can be improvised and standardized based on the defects trend derived from the analysis of such review comments and the type of errors found out of such reviews.

9.7 Most Common Errors Identified During Review

Possessing the knowledge of what could go wrong and how it could be prevented will enable the team to prepare better test cases. The following are the common areas where the test cases review could identify errors.

9.7.1 Coverage and Adequacy

- Incomplete test cases – For example, missing the crucial steps are in the test cases document that would hamper smooth the execution of the cases.

- Missing negative test cases – For example, covering only the explicitly stated requirements and not including the negative test cases that are implied by the requirement.
- Invalid test cases – For example, misinterpretation of requirements leading to invalid test cases

9.7.2 Test Data Related

- No Test Data – Not including test data as part of the test case. For example, specifying the input value as a positive value instead of giving the actual value.
- Inappropriate/Incorrect Test data – For example, including test data that is not valid for the scenario under test.

9.7.3 Correctness and Completeness

- Incorrect Expected behavior – Documenting the expected result incorrectly.
- Incomplete results/number of test runs – Not documenting the actual results and not tracking the number of test runs.
- Defect details not updated – Not updating the defect number, defect details against the failed test cases.
- Changes to requirements not updated in test case – Overlooking the changes made to the requirements subsequent to the test case preparation and not updating the test cases based on the changes.

9.7.4 Documentation Errors

- Grammatical errors and Typos
- Inconsistent tense/voice

It would help to identify the categories of these common errors and assign the categories to the review comments, so that the trend can be analyzed and necessary steps can be taken to address the frequently reported errors.

9.8 Key Benefits of Test Scripts Review

1. Factoring the review effort into the estimation helps in providing realistic estimates that would also ensure that the final deliverables are of desirable quality.
2. Following a defined process for testing cycle helps in standardizing the deliverables.
3. Streamlined review process and categorizing the findings would help in collating metrics related to the types of defects detected during the test cases review and analyzing these, would enable initiating corrective actions in the forms of training, tightening the requirements review process etc. as appropriate. The analysis of review results could be used for improving and standardizing the process.
4. The systematic approach to testing advocated here might increase the effort spent a little but the benefits would outweigh the cost by reducing the incidence of production defects significantly and by ensuring that the test cases produced are robust and highly successful in identifying defects.

9.9 Recap

- Review of test cases is very much pertinent in ensuring that they are correct, adequate and succeed in finding the obvious and latent defects in the Software.
- Streamlined review process and categorizing the findings would help in collating metrics related to the types of defects detected during the test cases review and analyzing these, would enable initiating corrective actions in the forms of training, tightening the requirements review process etc. as appropriate.
- Possessing the knowledge of what could go wrong and how it could be prevented will enable the team to prepare better test cases.

Chapter 10: Test Execution

Test execution phase involves actually running the tests that are intended to confirm that the system works as expected after the code is deployed in the test environment.

This is a crucial phase in the STLC. A lot of planning should go into the phase in order to ensure that the testing efforts are completed within the test execution schedule – which typically will be a much smaller timeframe within the SDLC. A detailed test strategy/plan should be created early in the lifecycle.

10.1 Test Execution Strategy / Plan

Test execution strategy or plan should elaborate in detail the following aspects with reference to the testing effort.

10.1.1 Number or Test Passes or Test Runs

The term "Pass" refers to the execution of the complete set of test scripts created to test a specific functionality or a set of functionalities in scope for the testing effort.

Typically, every testing effort will target to execute at least 3 passes of test execution – which essentially means that all the scripts created shall be executed at least 3 times during the test execution phase. This is to ensure that the defect fixes delivered do not impact the functions that were tested successfully in the prior pass.

10.1.2   Script Status Tracking

A script can be tracked under different status based on many factors. These statuses could be defined by the tool if one is used or it could be different for each organization. In general the main statuses are Pass or Fail but in addition there could be other statuses like blocked, deferred, de-scoped, not delivered, not executed, data not available to test etc. Assignment of specific status codes will help to track the pending scripts efficiently.

10.1.3   Detailed Test Execution Plan

Every testing project should target to create a detailed test execution plan that calls out the specific details regarding how the scripts/cases created shall be executed within the stipulated time. This should take into consideration the number of scripts, number of resources, number of days available for testing, number of scripts that each tester can execute per day and also provide for any factors impacting test execution to ensure that there is enough buffer in the plan to complete execution even if a few testing days are impacted by any issues like environment unavailability, resource unavailability, Code delays, data unavailability etc.

10.2 Test Execution – Entry Criteria

It is important to define and agree upon the entry/exit criteria for test execution and establish a process to validate that the entry criteria are met prior to test execution start date. A checklist to validate entry/exit criteria should be created based on the project needs and should be validated prior to each phase completion.

Some of Entry criteria items for test execution are given below:

- Test environment should be set up and accessible to the test team
- Code should be deployed in Test Environment
- Test scripts should have been created, reviewed and baselined
- Test data needs and identified and mapped to the test cases/scripts
- Test management and defect management tools and processes should be set up/created and shared with all stakeholders
- Test execution plan/strategy should be created, reviewed and shared with all the testers and other stakeholders
- Any critical defects identified from the earlier test phases like unit testing or Integration/Assembly testing done by the development team should be resolved

10.3 Test Execution – Exit Criteria

Some of Exit criteria items for test execution are given below.

- All test cases/scripts identified/planned should be executed. If there are exceptions, necessary approvals for not executing the scripts should be obtained
- All the test runs or pass executions planned should be completed.
- All the scripts executed should have passed the tests. If there are failed scripts, then exception for deferring the fix for the defects should be obtained
- All High severity defects should be fixed. Approvals should be obtained for exceptions

In addition, the test execution phase review checklist described in Chapter 8 should also be validated upon test execution completion.

10.4 Recap

- Test execution refers to actually running the tests intended to confirm that the system works as expected after the code is deployed in the test environment.
- Every testing effort will target to execute at least 3 passes of test execution
- Different statuses that can be assigned to test scripts to track them to closure are Pass, Fail, Blocked, Deferred, De-scoped, Not delivered, Not executed, Data not available to test etc.
- It is important to define and agree upon the entry/exit criteria for test execution and establish a process to validate that the entry criteria are met prior to test execution start date.

Chapter 11: Defects Management

Software development and defects co-exist since that their inception. Because of the project dynamics, complexity and other factors, it is next to impossible to prevent defects completely. Software testing as a field of expertise has evolved in order to ensure that the quality of the system is not significantly impacted due to this string bonding with the defects by identifying them early in order to get them fixed.

Managing the defect logging and tracking process and ensuring that the defects are tracked to closure is a vital task for everyone in the information technology team. Testers and developers should work closely to get the defects addressed in a timely manner.

11.1 What is a Defect Report?

A defect report is a very important deliverable that each tester should train to excel in creating. This report basically should convey the details about the problem in the system or a discrepancy between the requirement and the system behavior to the development team so that they can analyze the root cause and provide a fix.

An accurate, clear and concise description of the defect differentiates a good report from a bad one. Writing bad defect reports result in unnecessary effort overhead and should be avoided.

11.2 How to write a good Defect Report?

The following tips should be followed to write a good defect report.

1. Include a short and clear summary of the defect in the Headline. This should not be verbose
2. Include all relevant information about where and how the defect was found – environment, build/version, browser, operating system etc.
3. Provide a step by step description on how to recreate the defect
4. Include the actual result when defect was found and the expected result based on the requirements within the description clearly as separate sub sections
5. Include the test data used while the defect was found
6. Provide screenshots of the page or screen where the defect was observed
7. Provide additional information, if possible in the form of database query results, screenshots from the backend systems etc if discrepancies are noticed
8. Include any other information that would help the developer identify the problem quickly. For example, if you know the root cause of a similar defect include that as a comment
9. Get the defect report reviewed by a peer or the lead to ensure that invalid defects are not logged
10. Check if a similar defect is already created by other testers before logging the defect on the tool

11.3 Contents of a Defect Report

1. Defect Number
2. Defect Summary Headline
3. Tester Name
4. Defect submission date
5. Application under test
6. Defect identified in Build # or version #
7. Function under test
8. Sub function, if applicable
9. Environment – Operating System/Browser etc
10. Test Case/ Test Script reference
11. Defect Status (New, Under Analysis, Under Construction, Ready for Test, Closed, Implemented etc.)
12. Detailed Description of the defect
13. Step by step description to recreate the defect
14. Test Data used
15. Screenshots of pages showing the defect
16. Defect Severity (based on impact to the system/testing)
17. Defect Priority (based on the urgency of the fix)
18. Developer Name
19. Root Cause
20. Fix Details
21. Date Fixed
22. Fixed in Build # or version #
23. Retest Details

24. Retested By
25. Retest date
26. Detailed Comments

11.4 Defects Classification

It is important for a tester to be aware of how to assign severity to the defects. Severity indicates the level of impact of the defect on the software or testing of the system. Though the defect classification levels may vary for each organization, some high level guidelines apply.

11.4.1 Very High Severity/Show Stoppers

Assign this severity when
- The system crashes
- Testing comes to a standstill
- Legal compliance issues
- There is no work around

11.4.2 High Severity

Assign this severity when
- Major function is not working
- An important requirement is implemented incorrectly
- An important requirement is not implemented

- There is no work around for the function
- Testing can continue for other areas

11.4.3 *Medium Severity*

Assign this severity when

- A minor function is not working
- There is a workaround
- A portion of a function is impacted
- Incorrect Verbiage issues are found
- Testing can continue for other areas

11.4.4 *Low Severity*

Assign this severity when

- Cosmetic issues (UI, Layout etc.) are found
- Testing of functions is not impacted at all

11.5 Defects Management Tools

There are many defect tracking and management tools available that serve as defect repositories. Some of these tools are linked to the test management tools and these provide the ability to link the defect directly to a test case or test script.

It is important for a tester to get trained on the tool and understand all the features of the defect management tool well because this is one application that a tester will be using almost on a daily basis.

11.6 Defects Tracking Process

The tester should also be familiar with the defect lifecycle – the various statuses that a defect is moved to right from when it is logged to when it is closed. There can be multiple paths a defect can take based on the action required and root cause. The typical defect status changes are provided below. These statuses may vary by organization and the tool used.

11.6.1   Flow 1: Logged and Fixed

New – Analyze – Fix – Ready for Test – Fixed and Closed

This is the happy path – a defect is identified by the tester, analyzed by the developer, root cause found to be code related, fix is built and delivered, retested by the tester successfully and closed.

11.6.2   Flow 2: Logged and Fixed on second attempt

New – Analyze – Fix – Ready for Test – Not Fixed – Fix Again – Ready for test – Fixed and Closed

This is the alternate path – a defect is identified by the tester, analyzed by the developer, root cause found to be code related, fix is built and delivered, retested by the tester but not successful, assigned back to the developer for a fix and fix delivered again, tested by the tester successfully and closed.

11.6.3   Flow 3: Logged and Document updated

New – Analyze – Document update – Ready for verification – Document updated and Closed

This is another alternate path - a defect is identified by the tester, analyzed by the developer, root cause found to be a document update issue, System analyst fixes the document, tester verifies the updated document, confirms that the application behavior matches the updated document and defect is closed.

11.6.4   Flow 4: Logged and Closed as invalid

New – Closed

This flow should be avoided by the testers. Typically, this is applicable when the defect logged is invalid, duplicate or not reproducible.

11.7 Recap

- Managing the defect logging and tracking process and ensuring that the defects are tracked to closure is a vital task for everyone in the information technology team.
- An accurate, clear and concise description of the defect differentiates a good report from a bad one.
- Follow best practices while writing up the defect report
- Understand the contents of the defect report and the various flows in the defect cycle

Chapter 12: The Art of Error Guessing

There are various time-tested test cases writing techniques available for successfully finding defects. In addition to applying the techniques like Equivalence Partitioning, Boundary Value Analysis, Decision table testing, State Transition testing etc., it would be useful to adopt an innovative approach and come up with your own, custom-made defect detection techniques as well. Whether Error guessing is an art or science is a debatable topic but there is some scope to introduce a systematic and situation-based approach to it. Here are some tips that might come in handy.

12.1 Requirements Analysis

Identifying and eliminating most of the defects as early in the SDLC as possible must be the primary goal of a tester. Thorough requirements analysis is the most significant defect detection activity, aimed at identifying the flaws in requirements definition. Reviewing the requirements with the Tester's hat on and analyzing every requirement for its correctness and testability would help flush out any mistakes or ambiguities at a very early stage. Identifying the high impact defects at this stage would make the progress of the project smooth at the later stages.

12.1.1 Scope Analysis - Too Many Changes?

If a requirement contains multiple sub-divisions, then the possibility of missing out one of the components while coding is very high. So, more attention should be paid to ensure that each and every one of such components is tested so that any functionality misses and misinterpretations can be identified at the earliest. Similarly, if a requirement calls for change in more than one place – either in the code or in the User interface, the probability of finding a defect in one of these areas is higher.

12.2 Developer Analysis

Every developer has a working style - which if studied closer, would help you identify the defects pattern for each developer. This can be derived by analyzing the type of defects that have been logged and assigned to each of the developers against their code. By and large, it should be possible to categorize the working style of the developers into the following categories so that the testers can be more vigilant in the areas that are defects-prone as revealed by the defects pattern for every developer.

12.2.1   *Explicit Requirement is my Bible*

Some developers look only at what is stated in the requirement document explicitly. If a requirement that has implicit components is assigned to such a developer, it might help to dissect the explicit/implicit requirements and double check if all the implicit aspects have been considered. For example, if there is a requirement to modify the business rule while adding new customers – it is implicit that these business rules should be applicable while modifying the customer details as well. But some developers might overlook to update the Modify customer module as it is not explicitly stated in the requirement. When working with such developers, watch out for the hidden or implicit requirements and add test cases to cover such scenarios.

12.2.2 Content is minor

There are a few developers who do not pay much attention to the content as they consider that functionality or Business logic is more important. These people spend much of their energy in figuring out the correct implementation of the Business logic that they would overlook many content issues. It would help in these cases, to do a thorough checking of content along with functionality cases identified, to ensure that there has been no oversight.

12.2.3 One at a time approach

There are developers who are very thorough in their approach to a given requirement implementation and they block all possible loopholes in the module that are directly affected by the requirement. But many a time, even such detail-oriented people miss out on the implications of cross-module transactions. So, if you were working with such developers, concentrating more on the cross-module scenarios would help unearth possible defects.

12.2.4 Look and Feel – not my department!

Some developers often overlook the Look and Feel issues – especially since most of these are not specified in the requirements. So, if something is not aesthetically appealing or affects the look and feel of the user interface, they may not pay much attention. Hence, it would help to watch out for the look and feel or usability issues when working with such developers.

12.3 Situation Analysis

When there are too many players involved in the implementation of a requirement, there are more doors open for the defects to creep in. Let's take a simple example to illustrate this. If there is a requirement to generate a report containing a specific new data element – the database developer should create the field in the appropriate table and pass the details to the respective developer to be included in the code, the UI developer should create the Input field, the code should be updated to validate and capture this field correctly and save it to the database, the reports developer should ensure that the data is picked up from the correct location while generating the report. If anyone misses out or does something incorrectly or passes on incorrect information to the other party, it would be an open invitation for the defects. So, in such situations, testing should be done to catch the possible defects at each point of interaction.

These are a very few ideas on how to detect defects as early as possible given the constraints the testing teams are often faced with. However, many more techniques that are specific to the project team can be developed if the defect data is keenly analyzed and useful inferences are made out of such analysis.

12.4 Recap

- Know what to test
- Know the test phase
- Know your developers
- Know the development Organization

Chapter 13: Test Reporting

Reporting the status of testing effort to all the stake holders especially senior management is very important. For each testing effort, the type, purpose, frequency of the reports, recipients should be identified early in the cycle and they should be distributed to the identified stakeholders regularly. The reports should provide a detailed update on the key test metrics that reflect the current status of the effort.

13.1 Test Status Reports

Daily/Weekly/Monthly reports should be created to capture the status of the testing projects. At a minimum the below items should be included and additional sections could be added based on the project needs.

- Status Summary
- Detailed status update by Phase (Preparation, Execution)
- Issues requiring management attention
- Test Metrics and Graphs

13.2 Test Metrics

Testing metrics can be captured as the raw data such as the count of test scripts written, executed, passed, failed, count of defects logged etc. or they could be calculated metrics such as Defect Acceptance rate, Test Effectiveness etc.

13.2.1 Test Preparation Metrics

- # of Requirements
- # of Scripts Created
- # of Scripts Reviewed
- # of Test Data scenarios identified and mapped

13.2.2 Test Execution Metrics

- # of Test Scripts Executed
- # of Scripts Passed
- # of scripts Failed
- # of Scripts Pending
- % Execution completed
- Scripts Pass rate
- Scripts Failure rate

13.2.3 Defect Metrics

- # of Defects logged
- # of Showstopper defects
- # of High Severity defects
- # of Medium Severity defects
- # of Low Severity defects
- # of Defects Fixed and closed

- # of Defects Closed as invalid
- # of Duplicate defects

13.2.4 Calculated Metrics

Some of the calculated test metrics are given below. Additional metrics can be calculated based on the project needs.

- **Defect Acceptance Rate**

    Formula: Number of Defects Accepted and Fixed/Number of Defects Logged*100

    Increasing trend in the Defect Acceptance rate is the sign of project health being satisfactory. Decreasing trend would indicate a need to train the testers on the domain or application

- **Test Execution Effectiveness**

    Formula: Number of defects logged during testing / (Number of defects logged during testing + Number of Post Production defects)*100

    Increasing trend (towards 100) indicates that efficiency is improving. Decreasing trend indicates a need to provide additional training for the testers from an end user perspective

- **Test Script Effectiveness**

    Formula: Number of Scripts Executed/Number of Defects Logged

    This metric showcases the test script efficiency or the ability of the scripts to find defects. The value indicates that a defect is logged every so many scripts executed.

- **Test Script Creation Productivity**

    Formula: Effort spent on Scripts Creation / Number of Scripts Created

    This metric indicates the Tester productivity during Test Scripts creation. This should be looked at also taking into consideration the complexity of the scrip[ts

- **Test Script Execution productivity**

    Formula: Effort spent on Scripts Execution / Number of Scripts Executed

    This metric indicates the Tester productivity during Test Execution. This should be looked at also taking into consideration the complexity of the scrip[ts

- **Test Coverage Rate**

    Formula: Number of Scripts Created / Number of Requirements

    This metric shows the test coverage efficiency. The value indicates the average number of scripts written for every requirement

13.3 Recap

- Testing metrics can be captured as the raw data such as the count of test scripts written, executed, passed, failed, count of defects logged
- Calculated metrics such as Defect Acceptance rate, Test Effectiveness etc. help assess the efficiency of the test process

Chapter 14:   Key Levers to be a successful Tester

If you are a tester and want to turn your project into a success, here's a ten-point program that identifies the levers that will help to elevate the performance of the project from "Good" to "Great". These are some of the basic aspects that are often times overlooked unfortunately. But if the key points highlighted below are adopted and consistently followed by the project team, the overall success rate of the project would significantly increase and I've personally seen this work wonders.

14.1 Adopt a methodical approach to Testing

- Analyze the requirements and check if all the statements are clear and if all the required information is made available. If not, send a query and get the inputs. If there are any ambiguous statements, get clarifications for the same.
- Identify the required Test Scenarios in the Requirements Tracking Sheet ensuring that all the statements are covered.
- Ensure that all the scenarios identified in the tracking sheet are translated into test cases. Gather the test data required and if needed, seek the help from onsite QA team for the same.
- Get the test scenarios and Test cases reviewed by a Peer for test coverage, test adequacy and correctness.
- During test execution ensure that all failed cases are reported in the appropriate defect tracking tool and track every defect to closure.

- Capture the defect details and retest details in the Test case document. Ensure that while retesting the defects, regression testing is done on areas that could have been affected by the fix.
- For any changes in the requirements that have an impact on schedule/effort, escalate the same to onsite and get the approval from the concerned for revision of effort/schedule.
- After all the defects for a release are fixed, run the regression cases and integrity check for the release to ensure that the code tested earlier is intact.
- Run integrity check in Production on release date and ensure that all the requirements have been promoted successfully, report the findings and follow up on open issues, if any.

14.2 Ensure Schedule / Effort Adherence

- Get the information about the release schedule from the Managers and plan the activities in such a way that testing is completed without any schedule slippage.
- Always plan to complete work well within the effort estimate.
- If there are unanticipated issues like too many defects or changes in requirements that force an effort overshoot, escalate the same to the Project Manager and get the estimate revised by justifying the reasons as appropriate

14.3 Acquire the Business Knowledge

- Acquire the overall knowledge of the business, the application, the factors that affect various systems etc.

- Get a complete understanding of the key functionalities of the application being tested.

14.4 Maintain high Quality Documentation

- Prepare the test documents with the correct template. Ensure the correctness and completeness of all the contents before forwarding the document for review
- Ensure that all the deliverables are reviewed before delivery.
- Give all the required details without any ambiguity in every deliverable.
- Ensure that the documents are free of grammatical errors.

14.5 Adopt Just in Time Status Reporting

- Understand the Status reporting needs of the project, send the status of everyday activities to the concerned people without fail
- Ensure that the highlights of the day, number of defects, issues or queries etc are sent in these reports.
- If the answer to a query is not provided, mark the issue in bold in the status report on the following day. If the answer is not received beyond 2-3 days, mark the issue in bold red in the status report and escalate the issue to the next level managers.
- Send a consolidated weekly status report for those managers who would like to see only the essence of the weekly activities.

14.6 Track Issues to closure

- Report any issues or raise any questions through the status reports or via emails.
- Follow up till an answer or resolution is provided.
- If the answer is not provided mark the issue in bold in the status report. If the answer is not received beyond 2-3 days, mark the issue in bold red in the status report and escalate the issue to the next level managers.

14.7 Hone-up the Technical Skill Levels

- Work on honing the technical skills by requesting for training and keeping abreast of the current improvements in the area of specialization.
- Defects analysis can be done from a developers' perspective to learn about the root causes

14.8 Improve Communication and interaction

- Communicate and interact effectively among the resources in the project team and also from other relevant teams
- Escalate any queries to appropriate owners on time and follow up till the clarifications are received.
- Share with the team, any information that might be useful to the entire team or that might affect the team in anyway.
- Participate actively in the weekly conference calls
- Build a good rapport with the team members and managers.

14.9 Develop a keen eye for details

- If you find a typo on a billboard when you pass on by, you are on the right track to become a successful tester. Train yourself to look into the details and dig into the implicit aspects because software errors may not be as obvious as the typo on a billboard. Never assume anything and ask for documentation for all the test inputs.

14.10 Be Proactive

- Be proactive in seeking work, giving suggestions for improvement, taking up new initiatives, pointing to any issue that might affect the project in any way and be open to continuous process improvement.

Chapter 15: Tips to Write Effective Tests for GUI Objects

There are various types of objects used in any system and each of them have unique aspects that need to be considered while creating test cases to confirm that they are coded to accept valid values and generate errors for invalid values. Hence a tester should be familiar with the nuances of these various objects and also understand the specific focus areas for each object to provide adequate coverage in the test cases.

The tips below should help the tester get a better understanding of the different types of controls/objects and write more effective test cases for these objects.

15.2 Text Box

- The user should be able to enter values up to the maximum allowable length for the text box.
- If the user attempts to enter more than the maximum length, the keyboard entry subsequent to the maximum length should not be accepted.
- Entry of special characters should be validated appropriately.

15.2.1 Text Box - Date Field

- Any special dates should be validated properly.

- Date format should be validated. If a specific format should be followed instead of using a calendar utility to populate the field, a tip should be provided to the user indicating the correct date format.
- In specific scenarios, selection of future dates should be validated and suitable error message should be displayed.

15.2.2   Text Box - Numeric Field

- Entry of only numeric values should be accepted. Keyboard entry of alphabets should not be allowed.
- The entry of lowest and highest values in each of the valid ranges, the values above and below the highest and lowest should be validated.
- Entry of Zero should be accepted.
- Entry of invalid values should result in an error message.
- Leading blanks should not be accepted. Trailing blanks should be truncated.
- Negative values should be accepted where it is allowed.
- Any special values should be validated properly.

15.3 Radio Buttons

- Clicking on a Radio button with the mouse should select the item clicked.
- Only one Radio button should be selected at any time. If another button in the group is clicked, the item selected earlier should be deselected.
- Up and Down arrow keys should move the focus between the radio buttons in the group.

- Each group of radio buttons should have a default value in order to avoid situations where there may be a blank value retrieved from the database.

15.4 Check Boxes

- Clicking on the box with the mouse should make a check mark appear on the box. Clicking again on the checked box should make the check mark disappear.
- Selection of multiple boxes should be allowed.

15.5 Dropdown Menu

- Expanding the Arrow in the drop down menu should display the list of options.
- Scroll bars should be available if there are many options.
- Pressing any letter on the keyboard should display the first item in the list with that starts with that letter.
- All items should be in sorted in alphabetical order. Others/Blank/None options should be displayed at the top or the bottom of the Menu.
- Clicking on an item should select the value of the item as the value for the corresponding field.
- Default value should be displayed whenever a likely default choice can be identified.

15.6 List Box

- The list of values that can be selected should be displayed.
- Any item should be selected by clicking on the item
- Up/Down arrow keys should move the focus to the items in the list
- When an item is highlighted, clicking on Enter should select the item.
- Pressing any letter on the keyboard should display the first item in the list starting with that letter.
- Scroll bars should be available if there are many options.
- If multiple values selection option is available, a hint should be provided to the user indicating the same.

15.7 Command or Action Button

- Tab key should move the cursor to the Command button. Mouse click, clicking of Enter/space bar should activate the command button.
- Pressing <Enter> should activate the OK button <Esc> should activate the Cancel button on any page.
- If the action intended to be performed by the command button is completed, a confirmation message should be displayed. If the action intended to be performed by the command button is not completed, an error message stating the reason for not completing the action should be displayed to the user also prompting for rectifying the problem.
- Multiple clicks on Command buttons invoking actions should not be allowed. The button should be disabled after single click.

Chapter 16: Exercises

The aspiring testers should attempt to complete the below exercises in order to reinforce the learning from this book. You might want to go back to the chapters read again in case you are unable to make progress with these exercises.

16.1 Requirements Analysis Exercises

16.1.1 Analyze the requirement and identify the gaps

Application:

Online Order Processing System for Jewelry

Member Categories:

Silver, Gold, Diamond, Platinum

Requirement Description for Pricing Strategy for Gold Necklace:

Base price for While Gold Necklace is $75 and for yellow Gold necklace it is $85. First time members using the coupon code "FIRST" will get a 5% discount. Gold members will get a discount of 5%, Diamond Members will get a discount of 6%. Non-members will get no discount. Product pricing should be calculated and displayed correctly for each member on the application.

16.1.2 Analyze the requirement and comment on its validity

Application: Online Order Processing System for Jewelry

Member Categories: Silver, Gold, Diamond, Platinum

Requirement Description for Welcome Message:
Members should be able to access the online order web site using the URL www.orderjewelry.com. As soon as they launch the page, they should get a welcome message with their name and member type.

16.1.3 Analyze the requirement and comment on its clarity

Application: Online Order Processing System for Jewelry

Member Categories: Silver, Gold, Diamond, Platinum

Requirement Description for Member Login:
Members should be able to login with a valid username and password. If the username is correct then login should be successful. If the password is correct then the login should be successful. If user name is incorrect then error should be displayed. Platinum members can login without entering username or password using their special URL.

16.2 Test Script Creation Exercises

Complete the below exercises with reference to the online jewelry order processing system example given above.

Make some assumptions if the requirements are not clear for the purpose of this exercise but in real life scenarios, clarifications should be sought from the business/system analysts.

1. Create test scripts to validate member Login functionality
2. Create test scripts to validate the pricing strategy for the Gold Necklace

16.3 Test Data Optimization Exercises

Identify the different classes of data for the below test scenarios to ensure adequate coverage is provided for each applicable class. Use test data optimization techniques for this exercise.

1. Member Login scenarios
2. Pricing Strategy for Gold Necklace

Hint: Create the test data sets in tabular format

16.4 Defect Logging Exercises

Create a defect report for the failed scenarios given below and assign appropriate severity to each defect.

1. A Platinum Member logs in - Enters valid username - Invalid Password - No error displayed.

2. A Silver members logs in – Enters valid username and password, Welcome message displays member status as diamond

3. A first time silver member logs in – enters coupon code – looks up the product details for Gold Necklace – incorrect price is displayed

4. A member launches the URL – www.orderjewelry.com. – Page not found error is displayed

5. A Gold Member logs in – the welcome message displays member status as "Glod"

Good Luck and best wishes for a great software testing career!

Printed in Great Britain
by Amazon.co.uk, Ltd.,
Marston Gate.